Para Angela, por este encuentro
en la escuela y mi amistad, siempre fiel
Reina [illegible]
14 de abril 2010

La detención del tiempo / Time's Arrest

Reina María Rodríguez

translated by Kristin Dykstra

Factory School

La detención del tiempo / Time's Arrest

By Reina María Rodríguez
Translated by Kristin Dykstra

Essays by Kristin Dykstra and Roberto Tejada

Second Edition. Factory School, 2005.

ISBN 1-60001-996-X

Cover art: *Time's Arrest*, 2001, by Brian Collier.
Back cover: Reina María Rodríguez in Barcelona, 2004.
Photograph by Jorge Miralles.

For more information about Reina María Rodríguez and to hear audio recordings of her reading, please visit: factoryschool.org/reina

Factory School is a learning and production collective engaged in action research, multiple-media arts, publishing, and community service.

Contents

Vincent Van Gogh también pintó veleros

no sé cómo se construye un velero.
nadie me propuso nunca construir
un pequeño velero.
no traían más que tablas de salvación
para flotar a la deriva.
yo siempre te dije que era grande el océano.
tiene por imagen el viento y la madera
el viento del mar sin que nadie lo demande
lo encamina hacia mejores días
su seguridad es que el límite no existe
y la brújula no es más que un instrumento
para no perder.
antes sólo guiaban las estrellas
donde el hombre y el pez ponían sus ojos.
lo importante es la fuga del velero
su pasión por las olas
porque la travesía será larga
y la canción de las cítaras podría hundirnos
sin que lleguemos
a un faro inmóvil.

Vincent Van Gogh painted sailboats too

I don't know how you build a sailboat.
no one ever asked me to build
a tiny sailboat.
they brought only tablets of salvation, the boards
for floating adrift.
I always told you that the ocean was wide.
it has as its image the wind and the wood
the ocean wind, without orders from anyone,
channels the boat toward better days
its security exists in the absence of limitation
where the compass is an instrument for nothing more
than preventing loss.
before, only the stars were guides
where man and fish fixed their eyes.
the important thing is the sailboat's escape
its passion for the waves
because the crossing will be long
and the song of the zithers could drown us
before we arrive
at a stationary beacon.

conseguir un sombrero

con el sombrero viene el verano
y en el verano la yerba me sirve
para comprender a los hombres. ando por ahí
regada entre mis ojos y la cerca.
con el verano sofocante cambia el ritmo
y los pájaros hacen su espiral triunfando
despúes el nido. no se detienen
trabajan para mí desde lo alto.
llego en mi bicicleta con las piernas húmedas
aún del agua helada del río
y con esta canción que hay en mi boca
todavía soy una mujer cerrada
pero mi piel oscurece como los mirlos.
conseguir un sombrero a toda costa
para guardar un rostro que quiere detenerse y olvidar
el invierno. empezar el día
bajo las nubes bajas mientras los pájaros
desde lo alto murmuran la canción
que está en mi boca y pican la matriz
de esta mujer oscurecida
secándose los sucesos de ayer como si no existiera
más pasado que el día
mordiendo la espiral de los pájaros.
así se hará el nido en el verano.
no de la trampa de los pájaros muertos
en el viento
no de las anunciaciones creadas por la pérdida de sus alas.
no de la tormenta que aflojará la calma
hasta que llueva sobre sí.

getting a hat

with the hat comes summer
and in the summer, the grass helps me
to understand men. I walk there,
watered between my eyes and the fence.
with the suffocating summer, the rhythm changes
and the birds spiral, victorious
afterwards, the nest. they aren't slowed
they work for me up there.
I arrive on my bike with legs still wet with
the river's icy water
and with this song that's in my mouth
I'm still a woman closed off
but my skin darkens like the blackbirds.
getting a hat at all costs
to protect a face that wants to stop and forget
the winter. beginning the day
under the low clouds while the birds
up there murmur the song
that's in my mouth and peck at the womb
of this dimmed woman
drying off from yesterday's happenings as if nothing existed
but the day,
biting at the birds' spiral.
this is how the nest will be made in the summer.
not out of the snare of dead birds
in the wind
not out of annunciations arising from the loss of their wings.
not out of the storm that will abate the calm
until it rains over itself.

en el marco de la puerta

en el marco de la puerta
no hay luz ni sombra
sólo el vacío que nos precipita a la escalera.
a veces me lanzo por la baranda
para que el aire me rompa la cara
cierta alegría de alborotar
el pasamanos de mármol con mis piernas.
si hubiera sido un muchacho tal vez
sería futbolista   para concentrar la fuerza
en una pelota y romper los cristales difíciles.
pero esta necesidad
esta paciencia de ser
y esperar
que el día pase
se desgaste en el lavamanos
y caiga gota a gota.
en el marco de la puerta se disminuye
lo que viene de afuera
se reduce la esbeltez de lo que esperamos
sea viento o aparición.
ahí debería conocerse al hombre
contra la espalda: la luz
antes de entrar y de salir
cogido en sus faltas
en su pensamiento al enfrentarse
al adversario.
yo pondría enredaderas
para saber cuando cae quién regresa
de la trampa
y no está soñando todavía
como si el pasamanos
fuera un caracol.

in the doorframe

in the doorframe
there's neither light nor dark
just the vacuum that hurls us toward the stairwell.
sometimes I rush up to double over the banisters
to break my face against the air
certain joy from rioting against
the marble handrail with my legs.
if I'd been male maybe
I'd be a soccer player   to concentrate my force
on a ball and smash it through fractious crystals.
but this necessity
this patience of existing
and waiting
for the day to pass
may expend itself in the sink,
falling drop by drop.
in the doorframe, what comes from the outside
diminishes
it shrinks to the slenderness of the thing we're awaiting
be it wind or apparition.
there, should come to meet the man
up against my back: the light
before entering and exiting,
grasped in his deficiencies,
in his thoughts when confronting
the adversary.
I'd lay out vines
to be alerted when someone falls, returning
from the trap,
no longer dreaming
that the handrail
is a conch shell.

alguien descubre una ciudad

alguien descubre una ciudad
en el apartado rincón
contra el invierno y las rocas fraccionadas.
descubre un lugar para volver
para estar siempre.
alguien que no me ha visto espiar
detrás de las colinas y los árboles
donde el ovejero azul con su perro
busca el laberinto de los pastos.
quizá no sea el Armana
pero él descubre una ciudad
en el abismo
con la sabiduría de la abeja noctura
profanando el alimento de su propio panal
y la paciencia de los que ven como los ciegos
en el sueño del tacto
un apartado rincón
una ciudad que no existe.

someone discovers a city

someone discovers a city
in the distant corner,
against the winter and broken rocks.
someone discovers a place to come back to,
to be there, forever.
someone who hasn't seen me out spying
behind the hills and the trees
where the blue shepherd, with his dog,
seeks out the labyrinth of pastures.
maybe it's not El Armana
but he discovers a city
in the abyss
with the wisdom of the nocturnal bee
profaning the food of its own honeycomb,
with the patience of those who see like the blind
in the dream's sense of touch
a distant corner,
a city that doesn't exist.

el dique

tengo perforaciones espacios que dejé
para ser reemplazada y ahora son imágenes:
nítidas imágenes de sus brazos y piernas
apoyados en mí que observo desde el muro
una figura intemporal mi cabeza
a la distancia de no ser más ella misma
derrotada contra el vacío para que rompa
el dique.
si creyéramos al fin que somos buenos actores
una compañía de cómicos que deambula
en su carromato de muerte buscando otra respiración.
si creyéramos algo
sería más perfecta la ilusión de verdad
en este desamparo
y la brocha furtiva para disfrazar los pormenores
por donde nos escapamos de la desilusión
los mismos comediantes que aspiramos a hacer
tales patrañas.
la vida también puede observarse desde el lado muerto
de los ojos
la vida puede ser casual
si te tocó el espacio no concedido
la mentira piadosa de esa mano que abre tu piel
y te consuela con lástima otra vez el vientre seco.
qué le vamos a hacer.
conservar la mentira es también un don de los payasos
y es difícil permanecer en la distancia que nos separa
del dique casi imposible romperlo
representar de vez en cuando otro papel
mientras el carro avanza
parecido a la vida parecido a la muerte
con el silencio de quien no quiere vencer
su verdadero papel en el trayecto.

the dike

I have perforations   spaces that I left
so I'd be replaced and now they're images:
sharp images of her arms and legs,
supported on me, that I observe from the wall
a timeless figure my head
at the distance of not being itself any more
beaten against the emptiness to break
the dike.
if we believed at the end that we were good actors
a company of comic performers wandering around
in a death-cart, looking for other air to breathe.
if we believed something
the illusion of truth would be more perfect
in this homelessness
the furtive brush to mask the details
where we escape disillusion
the same comedians who aspire to tell
such silly lies.
life can observe itself too, from the dead side
of the eyes
life can be accidental
if it were your turn for the unconceded space
the pious lie of that hand that opens up your skin
and pityingly consoles you again for your dry womb.
what are we going to do for her.
to preserve the lie is also a clown's great gift
and it's difficult to stay   in the distance   that separates us
from the dike   almost impossible to break through it
to play another role from time to time
while the cart moves on
resembling life resembling death
with the silence of someone who doesn't want to fulfill
her true role in this trajectory.

los frágiles espías

un polvo oscuro me ensombrece la mejilla
la boca   el asco   cómo cubrir el asco
la fragilidad de sus espías?
un polvo oscuro para cubrirlo todo
y pasar discreta sin que sepan que soy yo misma
con polvo oscuro cubriendo otro fracaso.
porque mis amigos   mis buenos amigos también
habían calculado:
estamos hechos de límites no de barcos
y mis buenos y bellos amigos se embellecen
para poner alambres de púas.
pero yo sólo tengo polvo oscuro y va a llover
y se caerá ese embadurnamiento y se pondrán
opacos ellos también.
no soy divina   ellos tampoco son divinos
pero los demás esperan encontrar todavía
dentro de nosotros.
de qué te puedo salvar sin un transplante
de cosas esenciales? cómo relacionar
tu búsqueda conmigo y no ser vendible?
demasiada subasta.
me rompe el asco la boca cuando despierto
y pongo serio polvo oscuro sobre la mejilla
aún inofensiva
polvo oscuro para resbalar gelatinoso
y ellos caen en la trampa mis buenos y fieles
amigos que me hicieron soñar y descubrir sus trucos
frente a este espejo donde me veo y también estoy
mirándoles tan frágiles   tan penosamente frágiles.
me lastima la manera de cometer sus crímenes
eran tan inteligentes al principio!

the fragile spies

a dark dust shadows my cheek
my mouth   the disgust   how do you cover up the disgust
the fragility of their spies?
a dark dust to cover it up
and pass discreetly without them figuring out that I am me
with dark dust covering up another failure.
because my friends   my good friends had also
calculated:
we're swelled with limitations not with ships
and my good and beautiful friends beautify themselves
to lay out cords of thorns.
but I only have dark dust and it's going to rain
and that smear will melt off and they too
will become opaque.
I'm not divine   they aren't divine either
but the others hope to find it still
inside us.
what can I save you from, without a transplant
of essential things? how can I relate
your search to me, without being for sale?
too much like an auction.
the disgust bursts out of my mouth when I wake up
and I apply grave dark dust to my cheek
still inoffensive
dark dust for sliding, gelatinous,
and they fall into the trap   my good and faithful
friends who made me dream and discover their tricks
facing a mirror where I see myself and I'm looking at
them too, so fragile   so painfully fragile.
the way they commit their crimes offends me
they were so smart at the beginning!

plantagenet

M. Lowry

plantagenet ha vuelto con su barco vacío: plantagenet, plantagenet. un apellido ilustre, inglés, muy antiguo. acaso existió? la mitad de sus pies están mojados y trae en la mano la botella vacía. me ha derramado la otra mitad de su ideal a la cabeza, mescal y sueños. qué importa que los demás no vuelvan. mi único personaje: lo perseguí en el desierto y mis hijos —sus volcanes—, se hubieran llamado así: popocatépetl y amecaameca ... esto me ocurrió cuando tenía 14 años y una postal donde una niña, sentada de espaldas a la cámara, sobre la yerba, los miraba crecer ... no era yo y era yo misma: popocatépetl ... amecaameca ... pero volcanes al fin, se hicieron piedra, lava, y presencié el incendio de los bosques, donde ahora tengo este lugar de arenas dormidas y a veces violentas también, donde plantagenet pone su carpa, su botella y su desesperación: porque ya no necesita confiar ni poseer. han visto desde una capa de algodón una vagina arder, sangrar? pero era nieve la cúspide de ese otro volcán arruinado dentro de mí para siempre. era fin de mes y había luna llena. cuando tenía 15 años, un poco después, compré unas medias "Casino," en una caja de terciopelo verde, para mi papá ... pero él se fue en un barco oscuro y desapareció. con qué derecho fingir a esperar por los que vuelven? desde entonces, que no tuve esos hijos y ese padre, me convertí en impresionista ... no aplaces, no aplaces—me dicen aún sus voces: de este lado se puede morir muchas veces, quedarse despierta y dormida, echada y sola sobre la memoria. plantagenet ... te llamo pero no necesito sonidos, no tengo que expresar un código siniestro para que aparezcas, te has hecho sensación dentro de mí: los personajes son más ciertos, uno no muere por ellos, no necesitan otros espacios, estereotipas, no tienen que fingir, que seducir, que demostrar. cuando tenía 20 años, creía en Alamar como la antigua Grecia y me disfrazaba para invocar a sus dioses, aunque Baco se conformaba con un vino de seis pesos, mientras hacíamos anfionías: quiero decir, que recogíamos objetos extraviados y otros que no tenían un uso definido y los convertíamos en suerte. el que hizo de muerte aquella vez desapareció un día bajo una capa de talco y nos dejó ese sabor de la muerte joven. desde entonces fuimos desconfiados, inconsecuentes, lúcidos y extravagantes y de alguna manera —alguien— con su varita mágica o de pescar, nos hizo la vida fácil, indefinida de todo, hasta de lo indefinido ... "dios mío, es el horror —ha dicho plantagenet esta mañana—, y está acechándonos, los fantasmas sobre las persianas, las raquetas de nieve escarlata, el rumor de las oportunidades perdidas, y toda la furia, la angustia, el remordimiento, las voces, voces, voces ... las fachadas de ladrillos —de azufre—acusando como jueces, las interminables, pero —¿ay!— inexistentes conversaciones terapéuticas confirmando el diagnóstico y apuntando una solución, una vía de escape hacia la luz del amanecer ... el horror, no hombre, ni mujer, ni bestia, asomado a la oscuridad donde tañen las campanas ..." ha dicho él a mi oído, vuelto del hospital desierto, hinchado por las drogas y embotado como si anduviera dentro de una niebla espesa, los demás pensarán que hablo sola a ratos, que doblo la cabeza, pero no necesito a nadie más ... pequeño monstruo mío atormentado, de viaje por mi sangre y el mescal ... tengo 36 años de mala fama y soledad, me recupero a ratos ... la felicidad de la normalidad, los espacios que la vanidad ha ganado ¡qué me importan! ellos al menos perdieron la cordura antes que aceptar la dualidad, la crueldad del dolor, cortaste ya su árbol, tu oreja? yo fui expulsada del final por una operación semántica.

—ella llama a plantagenet, un apellido ilustre, inglés, muy antiguo. acaso existió?

—me preguntabas, a qué persona quería más?

plantagenet

M. Lowry

plantagenet has come back with his empty boat: plantagenet, plantagenet. an illustrious surname, English, ancient. he existed, didn't he? his feet are half-wet and he brings the empty bottle in his hand. he spilled the other half of his ideal over my head, mescal and dreams. what does it matter if the others aren't coming back. my only character: I pursued him through the desert, and my children —its volcanoes—, would have had these names: popocatépetl and amecaameca ... this happened to me when I was 14 years old and had a postcard with a girl, sitting with her back turned to the camera, on the grass, who was watching them grow ... it wasn't me and it was me exactly: popocatépetl ... amecaameca ... but volcanoes finally, they became rock, lava, and I witnessed the burning of the forests, where I have this place of sleeping sands now, sometimes violent, where plantagenet puts his tent, his bottle and his desperation: because he doesn't need to confide or possess any more. on a layer of cotton, have they seen a vagina burn, bleed? but the pinnacle of that other volcano, ruined within me forever, consisted of snow. it was the end of a month and there was a full moon. when I was 15, a little later, I bought some "Casino" socks, in a green velvet box, for my dad ... but he went away in a dark boat and disappeared. with what right, pretending to wait for people to come back? since then, not having those children or that father, I've become an impressionist ... don't postpone, don't postpone —their voices still tell me, you can die many times from this side, you can stay awake and stay asleep, expelled and alone on memory. plantagenet ... I'm calling you but I don't need sounds, I don't have to utter a sinister code for you to appear, you've created sensation inside me: the characters are more true, one doesn't die for them, they don't need other spaces, stereotypes, they don't have to pretend, to seduce, to demonstrate. when I was 20, I believed in Alamar like ancient Greece and I masked myself to invoke their gods, although Bacchus was content with a six-peso wine, while we were making antisymphonies: I mean, we collected stray objects and things that had no definite use and we arranged them haphazardly. what stood for death, then, disappeared one day under a layer of talc, leaving us the aftertaste of early death. after that we lacked confidence, we were inconsequential, lucid, and extravagant and somehow —someone— with his magic wand or fishing pole, made life easy for us, indefinite in every way, even in the very indefinition ... "my god, it's horror" —plantagenet said this morning—, "and it's all there waiting for us: the ghosts on the window blinds, the scarlet snowshoes, the whispering of lost opportunities, and all the fury, the anguish, the remorse, the voices, voices, voices ... the brownstone —- brimstone — fronts transformed into judges, the interminable helpful but —alas—nonexistent therapeutic conversations, clinching one's case and pointing a solution, a way out into the morning light ... the horror not woman, not man, not beast, glimpsed through the bell-sounding darkness ..." he said in my ear, back from the deserted hospital, swollen by the drugs and dulled as if he were walking around inside a thick cloud, the others will think that I talk to myself occasionally, that I bow my head, but I don't need anyone else ... my small tormented monster, traveling through my blood and the mescal ... my 36 years of infamy and solitude, I recover sometimes ... the happiness of normality, the spaces that vanity has earned, what do they matter! at least they lost sanity before accepting the duality, the cruelty of the pain, did you already cut their tree down, cut your ear off? I was expelled from the end by a semantic operation.

—she calls out to plantagenet, an illustrious surname, English, ancient. he existed, didn't he?

—you were asking me: which person I loved the most?

ascensión

Lenin

todos han muerto
debajo de estas bóvedas doradas
debajo de las piedras
se han consumido.
mi abrigo negro no puede guardar
el frío y las palomas cruzándome los pies
mi cuerpo blando bajo la luz de los íconos
entra en su foso
como si hubiera descendido
y me hundiera
sin ser iluminada.
el mundo sigue grande y sin descanso.
sobre la nieve sucia
los hombres te han amado
pero todavía no te han visto
completamente solo
sólo queda tiempo para caminar rápidamente
hacer la fila y las columnas de mártires
cepillarse los ojos con la pintura fría
para hacerlos brillar.
completamente solos
mis ojos y los íconos
no te ven
no oyen a dios a los artistas griegos.
si supieras qué sola estoy en la ascensión
me hace temblar bajo el abrigo negro.

ascension

Lenin

they've all died
under these golden tombs
under the rocks
they've been consumed.
my black jacket can't keep out
the cold and the doves walking across my feet
under the light of the icons my smooth body
passes their entrance
as if I had descended
and been submerged
with no illumination.
the world goes on, great and restless.
men have loved you
in the dirty snow
but they still haven't seen you
completely alone
there's just enough time left to walk quickly
to form the line and the columns of martyrs
to brush your eyes with cold paint
and make them shine.
completely alone
my eyes and icons
don't see you
don't hear god or greek artists.
if you knew how alone I am in the ascension
it makes me tremble under the black jacket.

indefinición

fui hecha
para merecer los espejismos.
un año con la cáscara de abedul
cortándome los dedos
pequeña para tanta belleza
perdida en la blancura de la nieve.
desayunábamos pepsi y manzanas
y caminábamos el palacio de invierno.
mi paso era seguro como el de Dostoievsky
y me detenía igual que él
dos veces ante la escalera.
toco la bruma y miro en los espejos
cansada   he venido a esconderme en la sirena de arcilla
que hay detrás de las puertas en invierno.
bájame.
el juego con flores significa la eternidad?
acaricio la cáscara de abedul como si fuera
tu mano y me escondo.
tenía el tiempo estas dos formas de ser
y yo me fui alejando alejando
hasta el final?
pero he oído que la bruma no termina
aunque te despiertes
será el principio?
froto la cáscara de abedul y dentro de mí
están los dos adolescentes
buscándose
con miedo a concluir frente al vitral
un acto
libre del peligro de las representaciones
y de las palabras   que persiguen el fin.

indefinition

I was made
to deserve illusions.
small for so much beauty
lost in the whiteness of the snow
a year with the birch bark
cutting into my fingers.
we were having Pepsi and apples for breakfast
and we were walking though the winter palace.
my step was as firm as Dostoyevsky's
and I paused just like him
twice before the stairs.
I touch the mist and I look into the mirrors
tired   I've come to hide inside the clay siren
that sits behind the doors in the winter.
get me down.
he loves me, he loves me not: does the game signify eternity?
I caress the birch bark as if it were
your hand and I hide.
time had these two ways of happening
and I went away away
to the end?
but I've heard the mist stays around
even if you wake up
is it the beginning?
I stroke the birch bark and inside me
are the two adolescents
looking for each other
afraid of ending up in front of the stained-glass window
an act
free of the danger of the representations
and of the words   that pursue the end.

oh, Sissi emperatriz

si pasara un mes sin mirarme
y después fuera otra
no estarían tan fijas   tan apretadas
las amarras.
no puedo ver más allá de la caricatura
y entrar en el círculo
en mi fábula con las princesas muertas.
oh, Sissi emperatriz qué engaño.
nos hicieron a gritos en los cuartos de hoteles
en las oscuras posadas de tránsito
en las camas de hierro donde se aferró
la inseguridad
la sangre del primer asesinato.
otro tono en los ojos y a disfrazarnos:
en las jabas llevábamos lo necesario para la función
alambre para mirar
rimel para las pestañas.
al toque de queda el bebé de goma bajaría
de un helicóptero con pico de cigüeña
estrangulándolo.
cogido en el experimento de soñar
observado en el microscopio
el desafío de vivir
en la poceta del baño en cuclillas
la intimidad.
oh, Sissi emperatriz
estoy segura que éstas son fallas del experimento.
vamos a poner un poco de gloria
o de incertidumbre
entre tu cuerpo y el agua.

o, Empress Sissi

if I went for a month without my reflection
and then I were some other woman
the cables   wouldn't be so steady
so tight.
I can't see beyond the caricature
or enter the circle
in my legend with the dead princesses.
o, Empress Sissi, what a fraud.
they made us, screaming, in hotel rooms
in dark lodgings
in iron beds where insecurity
lashed
the blood of the first assassination.
another tone in the eyes and to mask us:
in the bags we carried what we needed to attend the function
wire for seeing
mascara for our eyelashes.
when curfew sounded, the rubber baby would descend
from a helicopter, a stork's beak
strangling it.
taken in the experiment of dreaming
observed under the microscope
the challenge of living
on the toilet, squatting,
the privacy.
o, Empress Sissi,
I'm sure these are failures of experimentation.
we'll put a little glory
or uncertainty
between your body and the water.

espejos

... el creador del espejo envenenó el alma humano.
F. Pessoa

en los espejos, en los diferentes espejos: en el del baño, más alejado y casi siempre empolvado, jabonoso, roído por el agua; en el espejo de la caja negra y plástica de aquellos cosméticos de muestra que me regalaron en Chicago —y allí estoy de muestra, maquillada y vestida para la exposición, me miro. en el pequeño espejo ovalado infantil de madera, que por el envés es una flor, una margarita, con un rostro de niña dibujado en el centro, me miro y soy diferente a la otra, diferente en cada uno: hoy tengo 30 años, hoy acabo de nacer, hoy aprendo a caminar, a mirar ... cansada de buscar cosas imposibles, me he perdido en el laberinto de la realidad de los espejos. a veces toco mi cara allí, en el azogue frío, desdibujándose, y no me encuentro. también estuve de pie frente a un espejo largo y desnuda, pero allí había otras imágenes anteriores que no se perdían conmigo, otras imágenes que yo adquiría y rechazaba otra vez, porque no se parecían a mí. y entonces tú tocabas todas las formas del espejo y de las otras conmigo, qué me quedaba para entonces de distinta? fue una confusión aquella tarde entrar en aquel espejo de las deformaciones, donde en tu mente —y en la mente diabólica del espejo—, están todos los cuerpos anteriores, precipitándose, desaparecidos. pero ayer también supe que en los espejos que no aparece la imagen está el diablo y pensé, sin comentarlo contigo, en ese espejo opaco y profundo donde algunas veces contemplo mi ombligo y no aparece reflejada su imagen, sabes? y entonces, yo lo busco, lo busco, sin poder explicarme porqué desapareció de mi vientre con esa brusquedad y ahora sé que en mi ombligo es donde está el diablo: que allí se esconde la agonía de la apariencia, del nacimiento y la soledad, cuando me aburro de mirarme y no ser la verdadera causa de la contemplación en el tiempo que transcurre desde que mi primer ojo ve, hasta que el segundo, un instante ínfimo después, alcanza la refracción de esa imagen y siento la agonía de una forma que no conozco, que no me pertenece y no puedo pensar qué soy y quiero gritar, sacudirme y que alguien me salve de la sumisión de la apariencia, de esos espejos cóncavos, torcidos, subliminales, donde estamos metidos para vibrar por equivocación: ahora siento que alguna vez estuve allí, pero no estoy marcada. he olvidado el olor y la mirada de aquel camillero negro. sé que todo fue muy rápido y que yo me miraba por dentro en un espejo alto, redondo, que funcionaba como retrovisor y que esa vez yo me perdía definitivamente, me debilitaba por quedarme para siempre en ese espejo del lado contrario, aferrada a mi libro de Herman Hesse con las uñas. siento que la cara se me duerme, se me estremece y acalambra y que las piernas también están acalambradas, forzadas, que tengo la cara y la planta de los pies en ese espejo, y busco ... dónde está el diablo? y el ombligo que era pequeño, una ilusión en el centro de mi vientre, está tirando hacia afuera, hacia adentro, él me responde ... allí va a nacer de tu ternura y de tu maldad, allí está el diablo obsesionado siempre por el poder de la soledad y de los nacimientos. grité, abrí mucho los ojos y miré el reloj: no será el reloj negro de nuestra ceremonia, nunca será el reloj negro de lo eterno, pero tampoco el casual, el de lo efímero. en las esferas del reloj también me he visto, más plena, más normal, en el tiempo en que por detrás del abrazo todos corren a mirar el tiempo verdadero, mientras yo empujo, pujo, me retuerzo por encontrar ese otro tiempo sin manecillas ... sólo para locos. pero no es tu culpa, ni de los otros, es otra vez culpa del diablo que también va a nacer desde mi ombligo solo, desde su oquedad, desde su impaciencia sin reflejo en un espejo cualquiera y no luminoso: en un espejo partido y con los bordes ardientes, donde puedo decapitarme sin querer, o mirarme una expresión endurecida, menos líquida, menos frágil, aprendiendo esas cosas del diablo como todas las demás.

mirrors

> ... the creator of the mirror poisoned the human soul.
>
> *F. Pessoa*

in the mirrors, in the different mirrors: in the one in the bathroom, farther away and almost always dusty, soapy, gnawed by water; in the mirror inside the black plastic box for the display cosmetics that they gave me in Chicago —and there I am on show, made up and dressed for exhibition, I look at myself. in the little oval mirror for children, made of wood and shaped like a flower, a daisy, with a girl's face drawn in the center, I look at myself and I'm different than the other woman, different in every mirror: today I turn 30, today I've just been born, today I'm learning to walk, to look ... tired of searching for impossible things, I've lost myself in the labyrinth of the reality of mirrors. sometimes I touch my face there, unmaking itself in the cold mercury, and I don't find myself. also, I stood in front of a long mirror, naked, but there were other previous images inside that weren't getting lost along with me, other images that I acquired and rejected again, because they didn't look like me. and when you were touching all of the shapes in the mirror and the other women with me, what difference was left for me then? it was confusing that afternoon to enter the disfiguring mirror, where in your mind—and in the diabolic mind of the mirror—, are all of the previous bodies, rushing around, missing. but yesterday I also found out that the devil is inside the mirrors, where no image appears, and I thought, without discussing it with you, inside that deep, opaque mirror where I contemplate my navel sometimes, its image doesn't appear in the reflection, you know? and then, I go looking for it, I go looking for it, without being able to explain to myself why it disappeared from my belly so abruptly and now I know that my belly is the place where the devil is: that the agony of appearance is hidden there, the agony of birth and solitude, when I tire of looking at myself and of not being the true reason for the contemplation during the time that passes from when my first eye sees, until the slightest instant later when the second eye reaches the refraction of that image and I feel the agony of a shape that I don't know, that doesn't belong to me and I can't tell what I am and I want to shout, to shake myself off, for someone to save me from the submission of the appearance, from those concave, twisted, subliminal mirrors in which we're put to vibrate by mistake: now I sense that I was once there, but I'm not marked. I've forgotten the smell and the gaze of the black man bearing the stretcher. I know that everything was very fast and that I was looking inside with a tall, round mirror, which served as a rear-view mirror, and I know I lost myself definitively that time, I was weakening from staying always on the wrong side in the mirror, clinging to my Herman Hesse book by my fingernails. I feel my face falling asleep, it makes me shudder and cramp and I sense that my legs are also cramped, strained, that I have my face and my feet planted in that mirror, and I'm searching ... where is the devil? and the navel that used to be small, an illusion in the center of my belly, is pushing outward, pulling inward, he's responding to me ... there he'll be born out of your tenderness and your wickedness, where the devil is always engrossed with the power of the solitude and the births. I cried out, I opened my eyes wide and looked at the clock: it's not the black clock from our ceremony, it will never be the black clock of eternity, but it's not the accidental clock either, the ephemeral one. I've seen myself inside the faces of the clock, fuller, more normal, in the time behind the embrace, where everyone is running off to look at the real time, while I'm pushing, struggling, I writhe to find that other time without hour hands ... just for the insane. but it's not your fault, or theirs, it's the fault of the devil who will also be born from my only navel, from its cavity, from its impatience without a reflection in any unilluminated mirror, in a smashed mirror with burning edges, where I can decapitate myself without desire or look at myself with a hardened expression, less liquid, less fragile, learning those things about the devil like all of the other women.

con la pasión de Juana de Arco

qué importa el frío
si uno se inventa su calor en las palabras
que se van quemando
unas contra otras hasta el pelo que empieza
a arder con desesperación.
qué importa aquí sentada
minuto tras minuto
este frío y este calor alternándose
con la muerte y la luz:
la sensación de una espada en el silencio
corta mi lengua.
qué importa si la protección espanta al fuego.
puede ser que la noche acabe con su codicia
entonces
inventaré la llama.

with the passion of Joan of Arc

who cares about the cold
if you invent heat in the words
that burn,
some against others, up to your hair, which ignites
with desperation.
what does it matter, sitting here,
minute after minute,
this cold and this heat alternating
with death and light:
the sensation of a sword in the silence
slices my tongue.
what does it matter if the form of protection frightens the fire,
maybe the night will wrap its greed
and then
I will invent the flame.

la detención del tiempo

Falcón

será cierto que en un plano más alto todo puede ser eternamente coexistente? será cierto, que es sólo la conciencia, nuestra conciencia, lo que experimenta el transcurso del tiempo, que en el sueño no existe el tiempo y la causa y el efecto se confunden? tú crees que la mente inconsciente coexiste con el universo y que esa simultaneidad no es más, que una regresión mística. y en la torre, en esa prisión, aparezco yo. muchos han hablado de la flecha del tiempo, tú por el contrario, quieres saber de las cosas que perduran, algo así —como lo llamabas—, el círculo del tiempo: está la flecha del río que fluye, —sin la cual no hay cambio, ni creación; pero también está el círculo, la sucesión en sentido de instantes. tal vez esto no sea de gran interés para los físicos y sus aplicaciones prácticas, pero ese dilema del determinismo, está implícito en el pensamiento simultaneísta y también en el existencial: para mí es la memoria del agua y ahora sé que el agua tiene memoria (París 1988) ... y que jamás me libraré de esta costumbre que tengo de seguir el agua ... tiro una piedra al mar, al arroyo, al charco más pequeño y de ella saldrán círculos, vueltas, espirales, espejos: y en el fondo podrás contemplar y robarte las formas del agua. tú las miras, las quieres poseer, pero ellas se escapan, al fondo. las tendrás sólo un instante, el instante en que abres sus hondas para ver. el agua es transparente y te engaña, no todo lo que dejas caer en ellas es el olvido. como en "Las olas", de Virginia, la naturaleza humana cambia y sólo parece transformarse de la misma manera que partículas de agua movidas por una ola. entonces, tiro una piedra al mar y si soy simultaneísta, la piedra ya habrá golpeado y se habrá hundido antes de caer y si soy ciencista, nunca alcanzaré el fondo, porque tampoco alcanzaré el agua. a veces, quiero tirar piedras sin pensarlo más —sabiendo que es una estupidez y haciéndolo, porque así se hacen las estupideces. alguien ha dicho, que nuestro modelo del cosmos tiene que ser inagotable: ni la pura secuencia, ni la pura unidad para explicarlo. y yo quiero, como tú, una complejidad que no sólo incluya la duración, sino también la creación; no sólo el ser, sino el devenir, no sólo la geometría, sino la ética. no buscamos una respuesta, más bien queremos la interrogante, la obsesión por aquella pregunta, será cierta la detención del tiempo? ... y elijo tirar piedras sin pensarlo más y entonces tú te escondes, te escondes y duermes. pero tú no eres tú, tú eres la idea de muchos anteriores que han dormido también. cuando tú duermes, yo miro y toco con los ojos, los que murieron ya en ti alguna vez, muchas veces. tú duermes, y a pesar de la levedad de ese instante, sigo sin saber —y recurro a Shakespeare—, "cual sustancia es la vuestra, de qué estáis formado, para que en vos se reflejen millares de formas extrañas ..." y, cuando tu gran boca movediza se abre y todo parece calmarse, entrar, desaparecer —como si yo sintiera ese placer de lo que muy adentro, debajo de ese rictus, está pasando— entonces, pueden moverse los labios, los párpados, temblar y presentir que vas a venir de ese otro lado oscuro, pero eso tampoco es verdad. en realidad se ha detenido el proceso de existir —el círculo del agua más cercano—, y es maravilloso saber que alguien duerme frente a ti con la inocencia de la muerte joven: en ese momento todo depende de mí que estoy consciente y soy, que puedo ver tu hombro y los pequeños pelos rojizos dentro y los rayos que por la ventana han entrado a morirse también y forman franjas de luz sobre tu cuerpo oscuro ... cada uno, como uno que es tiene una sombra que le pertenece, pero vos que sois igualmente único, proyectáis toda clase de sombras ... esta es la gloria, la inmortalidad. o sólo la detención del tiempo: será cierto que entre Einstein y tú el tiempo puede detenerse? ... yo me quedo sobre la sombra y la duda otra vez, como un ser puramente eleático en la ingravidez, otra vez con las piernas en cruz, sobre las flores de mármol, otra vez convencida de la inmortalidad porque te veo, te veo, te imagino mientras amanece y se van apartando dentro de mí también las dudas y las sombras ... y el cuarto va creciendo y empieza a vencer la luz: apago tu lámpara. te vas quedando detenido en el tiempo de mi mano, en la figura que te hago al vacío, desde mi escondite de ser, hecha un ovillo, donde puedo ver lo que pasa dentro de tus ojos: están pasando del verde al amarillo, a un río grande con muchos afluentes ... y empiezo a mojarme, a temblar, es un temblor húmedo por donde están pasando también las olas del tiempo. y yo traigo un pozuelo caliente con una bebida extraña que tomaremos juntos, con un sabor fuerte y quemado que aprenderemos también y olvidaremos pronto, sentados y únicos en el centro, donde el humo me quema la boca, la nariz: estoy delgadísima, me vuelvo una hilacha de humo.

time's arrest

Falcón

is it true that on a higher plane everything can be eternally coexistent? is it true, that it's only the consciousness, our consciousness, the thing that experiences the passing of time, true that in dreams time doesn't exist, and cause and effect become confused? you believe that the unconscious mind coexists with the universe and that the simultaneity is nothing more than a mystical regression. and I appear in the tower, in that prison. many have spoken of the arrow of time, in contrast, you want to know about the things that endure, something like that —as you were calling it—, the circle of time: the arrow is in the flowing river, —without which there's no change, or creation; but the circle is there too, the succession, in the sense of instants. maybe this isn't especially interesting for the physicists and their practical applications, but that dilemma of determinism, it's implicit in simultaneist thought and also in existentialism: for me it's the memory of the water and now I know that the water has memory (Paris 1988) ... and that I'll never free myself from my habit of following the water ... I toss a stone into the ocean, into the stream, into the smallest puddle and out go circles, circuits, spirals, mirrors: and in the depths you can ponder the forms and steal them out of the water. you look at them, you want to possess them, but they escape to the bottom. you'll only have them for an instant, the instant when you open up their depths to see. the water is transparent and it fools you, not everything that you drop into its forms is lost in oblivion. how in The Waves, Virginia's, human nature changes, only seeming to be transformed, like particles of water moved by a wave. then I throw a stone at the sea and if I'm a simultaneist, the stone already will have hit and it will have sunk before falling and if I follow Zeno, I'll never get to the bottom, because I'll never get to the water. sometimes, I want to throw stones without thinking about it anymore —knowing that it's inane and doing it, because that's how you do inane things. someone said that our model of the cosmos must be inexhaustible: neither pure sequence nor pure unity to explain it. and like you, I want a complexity that doesn't just include duration, but also creation; not just being, but becoming, not just geometry, but ethics. we aren't looking for an answer, we'd rather have the obscurity, the obsession with that question, is it true that time can be suspended? ... and I choose to throw stones without thinking about it anymore and then you hide, you hide, you fall asleep. but you aren't you, you're the idea of many others who've slept before. when you sleep, I look at them and touch them with my eyes, the ones who already died inside you once, many times. you sleep, and in spite of the levity of that instant, I go on without knowing —here I resort to Shakespeare—, "what is your substance, whereof are you made, that millions of strange shadows on you tend ..." and, when your great moving mouth opens and everything seems to grow calm, to enter, to disappear —as if I feel that pleasure of what is happening, deep inside, under that grin— then, they can move their lips, their eyelids, they can tremble and foresee that you'll come from another darkened side, but that isn't true either. in reality, the process of existing has been suspended—the closest circle in the water—, and it's marvelous to know that someone is sleeping in front of you with the innocence of early death: in that moment everything depends on me, that I'm conscious and that I exist, that I can see your shoulder and the little red hairs and the rays that have entered through the window to die too, forming bands of light across your dark body ... every one hath, every one, one shade, and you, but one, can every shadow lend ... this is the glory, the immortality. or only time's arrest: is it true that between Einstein and you time can be stopped? ... again I remain like a purely Eleatic being in weightlessness, above the shadow and the doubt, with my legs crossed again, above the marble flowers, convinced again of immortality because I see you, I see you, I imagine you while dawn breaks and the doubts and the shadows are withdrawing inside me ... and the room is growing and the light begins to win: I turn off your lamp. you stay, arrested in the time inside my hand, in the figure that I make of you at the edge of the void, from the hiding place where I'm curled up in a ball, where I can see what's happening in your eyes: they're changing from green into yellow, into a great river with many tributaries ... and I start to sweat, to tremble, the tremor is wet, in it waves of time go rolling past. and I bring a jug containing a hot, strange drink for us to share, with a strong burnt flavor that we'll learn to recognize and quickly forget, we are seated and unique at the center, where the smoke burns my mouth, my nose: I'm extraordinarily thin, I unravel like a thread of smoke.

Translator's Note

(Revised & Expanded for Second Edition, 2006)

Kristin Dykstra

Reina María Rodríguez was born in Havana in 1952. As a college student she took a degree in Latin American literature at the University of Havana, where she won the university's March 13th writing contest and began to spend time with other writers. Since then, in addition to publishing many books of different and often experimental genres, Rodríguez has collected a series of impressive honors, including two Casa de las Américas prizes for poetry and the Italo Calvino award for her first novel. She continues to live in Havana today in a rooftop apartment with her teenaged daughter, Elís, and her partner Jorge Miralles.

The poems printed in *La detención del tiempo / Time's Arrest* are selected from her 1992 collection, *En la Arena de Padua* (UNEAC). In these poems Rodríguez first felt that she had learned to negotiate two strands of her poetic voice, blending conversationalism's everyday imagery and tone with the defamiliarizing tones of philosophical thought. The poems in *Time's Arrest* thus represent familiar sights, such as human bodies, but it presents them in semi-alienated ways. Bodies are stretched, twisted, and compressed as if moving through funhouse mirrors. The recurring mirror images themselves morph into other surfaces: water, perception, time. Life appears in irrational and mythic forms, versions explicitly associated with insane or at least *un*-"sane" realities.

The distortion of time—its suspension emphasized in this collection's title poem, "Time's Arrest"—allows for a return from estrangement to the everyday world of conversationalism. Individual poems present familiar objects and people comprising the speakers' daily lives (hats, doorframes, Pepsi, clocks, mirrors, one's own face or body, friends, and so forth). Yet as Roberto Tejada discusses in the essay included in this edition, Rodríguez is aiming for a mark beyond the form of Cuba's 70s-era conversationalism, working to fuse and unsettle its propositions with increasingly postmodern sensibilities.

In Rodríguez' hands the combination of everyday things and their distorted twins results in a dark and fractured beauty, as in the poems "mirrors" and "the fragile spies." This tendency to darkness and distortion has led reviewers such as Duanel Diaz to call Rodríguez' writing a poetry of crisis. [1] Yet in keeping with Tejada's reading of vital community energies that forwarded paradigm shifts of the 1980s, Diaz links the poetry's conceptual crises with productivity rather than despair: in crisis he finds Rodríguez' most intense loyalty to critical thinking, the center of a poetics exploring the simultaneous construction and deconstruction of perception is essential to life. In *La detención del tiempo / Time's Arrest*, hallucinations and fragmentation coexist with the hopeful determination heard in "with the passion of Joan of Arc." Meanwhile, "time's arrest" suggests the achievement of a thoughtful state, a prolonged meditation in which "cause and effect become confused," suggesting that new perceptions of the past, present, and future can (perhaps must) be created.

Rodríguez builds these alternate realities not only out of her original voice and thought but by trying on other writers' perceptual lenses, a fact which has influenced the language of my translations. Tejada discusses the influence of José Lezama Lima, whose importance to Rodríguez cannot be overlooked. English-language writers are also part of Rodríguez' frame of reference: both Virginia Woolf and William Shakespeare appear in "time's arrest," and not just where they are named, so my use of English derives in part from readings of their texts. Furthermore, years after finishing a translation of "plantagenet," I recognized some of its odd language while reading Malcolm Lowry's *Lunar Caustic*. The revised 2005 translation takes this intertextuality into account by incorporating more of Lowry's exact words, although Rodríguez did alter his language slightly in her appropriation (for example, "it's all there waiting for me" becomes "it's all there waiting for *us*").

Rodríguez has described her writing process from the 1990s as processes of deliberate "recycling" (email, 1/11/2005, my translation). With this in mind, a great pleasure in reading her poetry can come from finding these recycled English-language texts and thinking about what (if anything) it means to recycle them. The dialogue that Rodríguez uses for *her* Plantagenet comes from a conversation between Lowry's protagonist, Bill Plantagenet, and his doctor at a psychiatric hospital in New York City. So does the recurring imagery of boats. Awakening in the hospital, Lowry's disoriented Englishman first identifies himself as the S.S. Lawhilll (13) and is called "the man who thought himself a ship" (21).[2] As his fogs begin to dissipate, Plantagenet realizes that he is a man but believes that he is *on* a ship. When this impression also passes and the reality of the urban hospital crashes in upon him, boats come to represent his search for a reality not constrained within the horrors of hospitals, wars, and pain: "Where were all the good honest ships tonight, he wondered, bound for all over the world?" (65) Rodríguez remarks that writing her own "plantagenet" allowed her to reflect on states of freedom and constraint, as well as the arbitrariness of the labels used to delimit psychological states: "That's normal, this one's crazy."[3] She remembers that she was so taken with the "unforgettable" *Lunar Caustic* that she presented a copy to Miralles, who eventually used Lowry's text as one of the sources for his short story "La ballena."[4]

The discussion of "plantagenet", opening up the thematics of freedom and limitation, reveals issues at play through *En la Arena de Padua*. While these reflections about freedom clearly tap into international literary conversations, as exemplified by the very citation of *Lunar Caustic*, it is simultaneously significant that Rodríguez' book was published early in Cuba's Special Period, a time of extreme hardship that followed the loss of the Soviet Union's economic and political support. Historian Jorge Domínguez notes that deepening economic troubles and the return of Cuban troops to the island (often following successful campaigns abroad) combined to diminish the nation's status: "If for thirty years Cuba had been able to behave as an unlikely 'superpower,' by the early 1990s it had once again become just an island in the sun" (in *Cuba: A Short History*, 147). In the context of the early '90s, Rodríguez' poetic imagery of isolation, disillusionment, entrapment, and surveillance becomes particularly complex. The connections of the past have not vanished entirely; she maintains reference to the Soviet Union, mediated through imagery of her remembered travels (for example to the Winter Palace) and including an elusive invocation of Lenin at the opening of a poem, which could be read either as a celebration or critique of martyrdom.

Rodríguez' use of intertextuality and references to the comings and goings of ships gives her a wide range of symbolic potential across her different book projects. She is clearly interested in metaphysical issues. At times the reader may also connect her poetry to specific island cultural conversations about around eclecticism, identity, and the travels of people to and from the island. Artist and writer Coco Fusco observes,

> During the 1980s, debates around eclecticism as a constant in Cuban art history broadened the parameters of what could be considered national culture. By stressing that Cuban culture was an amalgam of foreign influences, astute Cuban artists and critics won over bureaucrats who sought to restrict Cuban art to murals, documentary photographs, and sculptures of guerrilla heroes and revolutionary "new men." However, migration remained taboo because it suggested there existed a Cubanness beyond the island, an affront to a political ideology that relies heavily on nationalism and territorial defense for its sense of identity. No significant work ever circulated publicly, for example, about the 1980 Mariel boatlift in which 125,000 people left the country in weeks.[5]

1980 was not the only moment of highly visible departures of boats from the island, Fusco emphasizes:

> In the five years before the 1994 rafter crisis, several thousand Cubans left the island in jerry-built boats and rafts, with nearly a third of them perishing at sea. For years, this slow hemorrhaging was not publicly acknowledged in Cuba. Yet as early as 1992, the painter Carlos Rodriguez Cardenas, then in Mexico, broke the silence with his "Monumento a los Caidos" (Monument to the Fallen) depicting a sunken raft hovered

over by Cuba's patron saint. (160)

Fusco discusses artists as prominent as José Bedia and Kcho (Alexis Leyva) who have also taken part in this visual conversation since 1992, often but not always showing their work about boats and rafts outside the island.[6]

At the beginning of Rodríguez' poem "Vincent Van Gogh painted sailboats too," a poem included in this collection, the speaker's reflection on not knowing how to build a boat references the improvisational construction of boats and rafts that carried thousands of people to life and death offshore. Fellow poet Ricardo Alberto Pérez asserts the historical importance of her early use of raft imagery in his introduction to her 2003 book *Otras cartas a Milena*, noting that while today Kcho has become internationally famous for delicate sculptures of rafts, Rodríguez was among those who produced artistic riffs on the subject very early on and should not be perceived as merely following in Kcho's wake when she returns to imagery of rafts and boats, entrapment and liberation, life and death. As I have noted, it is important to read Rodriguez' 1992 poems reprinted in *La detención del tiempo / Time's Arrest* for many other sorts of meaning aside from political debates. However, one of the most striking features of her poems can best be appreciated by situating it in sociopolitical contexts: the way their moments of isolation and lyric individuality melt into fraught conversations about community—and back out of them.[7]

Like other Cuban writers of her generation, Rodríguez has stated that she assumes the self to be inherently social rather than private. Perhaps this is the most general reason why her writing often seems charged with a public and historical vision despite its overtones of isolation and intimacy. If the island *chisme*, or gossip, says any number of things behind closed doors in a way that's both powerful and indirect, then it might be said that Rodríguez' poetry adopts a similar manner of speaking about issues affecting both her daily life and her understanding of aesthetics.

No account of Rodríguez' career can dispense with an account of the work that she has put into creating a site for alternative cultural discourse, hosted at her home for over two decades. *La azotea de Reina* (Reina's rooftop) has served as a contemporary site for tertulias, the social gatherings that have been important to the island's intellectual culture since the colonial era. Furthermore, Diaz notes that Rodríguez, like her predecessors Dulce María Loynaz and Fina García Marruz, makes her home both a site of writing and a source of writing. Yet Rodríguez treats domestic imagery in a unique way. Diaz writes, "Reina's home is filled by the world outside it: the neighborhood, the racket from the street, the rooftop's tempting abyss. Inside and outside intertwine, as in her poem 'luz acuosa,' where the city invades the view from the azotea and everything grows to be threatening, estranged."[8]

The role of the azotea in relation to official Cuban cultural institutions continues to shift over time. It is the primary referent in the title of the literary magazine, *Azoteas*, first published in Cuba in January 2001 under the auspices of the Instituto del Libro. The editors — Rodríguez and Antón Arrufat, with assistance from Jorge Miralles — celebrated the release of *Azoteas* in Havana during an international festival organized in conjunction with the Instituto del Libro. Suggestively, the cover photograph for the magazine's first issue shows a child with a Cuban flag painted on his forehead. The photo has been scanned onto a piece of paper that lifts to reveal text. Here I include part of the manifesto printed under the child's photograph:

> *Azoteas* performs this simple experiment: to place a figure in an open space, a space without walls that stretches toward the horizon, in search of other figures on other rooftops. Cuban writers and artists are dispersed: when two in Mexico City or in Madrid, in Miami or in Havana, refer to a third and absent person, they lend him life. Cuban culture will not be able to limit itself to the figure on the island. Increasingly, it will have to respond to a destiny of dispersal. The trustworthy maps of a culture are those of its imaginary cartographies, which describe the lives of its writers and artists, traveling in order to find the same country in others.

> A magazine of Cuban literature circumscribed at a border marked by a coastline would result in a paralyzing reductionism. Along the same lines, to believe that the country ended at a set date — 1959 — and to consider that what continues here is a bothersome hiatus in history, is equally reductive. A living culture cannot be caught in traps of time or space; it leaps beyond them.

At a meeting with festival participants following the release of the magazine, Cuba's Minister of Culture, Abel Prieto, asserted that the *Azoteas* group's cultural work was consistent with the work performed in the state's official spaces, citing shared values of resistance and artistic quality. On the part of the editors, though, there was a sense at the festival that *Azoteas* could not be assimilated so easily. The palpable tension is consistent with a trend in recent Cuban writing remarked by James Buckwalter-Arias: writers' stated needs to resist state cultural institutions, sometimes paired with a simultaneous desire to resist pressures exerted by economic markets and/or to recuperate older theories of art as an apolitical practice.[9] In the case of *Azoteas* in 2001, Arrufat replied to Prieto's official rhetorical embrace of the magazine with an equivocal, "We'll see. This arrangement may not be permanent." In our own conversations, Rodríguez has described the magazine's relationship with the Instituto del Libro not as a consistent formal or ideological structure but as an arrangement made possible by a dear, long-time friend. As of mid-2005, the editors continue to work at getting issues of the magazine out, though at erratic intervals.

When I first agreed to do the first edition of this chapbook, I specified that Rodríguez' work should be reprinted with my translations. In the translator's note for that first edition, I commented on the difficultly of finding Rodríguez' poetry in the original, both in Cuba and in the United States. In 2005 I can now offer updates on the availability of her work. On the island her books still sell out quickly,[10] and Rodríguez still gives away all of her own copies of her books. She continues to actively write and publish new work in Havana: in 2003, for example, Ediciones Unión published *Otras cartas a Milena*, and her collection *Bosque Negro* was published in 2005 by Ediciones Extramuros. She hopes to see her *Libro de las clientas* published early in 2006.

In the United States, where this collection is published by Factory School, Rodríguez' work has become easier to find in recent years. Libraries are collecting her work published in Cuba and elsewhere; Princeton has started an archive of Rodríguez' work that includes delicate handwritten letters and notebooks. Green Integer Press published the anthology *Violet Island and Other Poems* in 2004. Translations of her poems by Nancy Gates Madsen, Roberto Tejada, and me have been published in a variety of magazines. Bilingual offerings appear online at *MiPOesias* 19:3 (www.mipoesias.com) and *Fascicle* (www.fascicle.com), and Factory School has posted Spanish-language audio recordings of Rodríguez in its archive of poetry readings (http://factoryschool.org/pubs/cuban7/index.html) which have been archived a second time by the University of Pennsylvania (http://www.writing.upenn.edu/pennsound/x/Rodriguez.html).

What does this mean for Rodríguez? Not a sea change, certainly: given her professional accomplishments, she was already known to specialists in Latin American literature in the United States. They have been arranging visits to the rooftop for informal and formal events ever since she began to host events there. However, circulation of her work in the US may point to present and future transitions in her readership, and not only in traditional print forms. She has begun to receive more invitations from U.S. universities to give readings, although she is not able to predict whether or not she will be permitted to enter the country to follow through on some or all of those invitations in the future.

The internet is both present and absent as a tool for Rodríguez. In March 2005, while in Havana, I discussed the rise of online literary activities in the United States with Rodríguez and Miralles, who both have access to email but not to the internet. They were very interested in this topic. Many of their fellow writers in the city have partial or regular access to email at this point but cannot work with the internet due to tight restrictions on its use, although tourists may not perceive the importance of those restrictions because they can buy time slots on computers with internet access at the more luxurious Havana hotels. In the United States, online magazines represent a new, often cost-effective way for poets to reach relatively broad audiences; by contrast, Rodríguez can't see even her own publications at *MiPOesias* or *Fascicle*, nor can she share them with anyone in Havana. She can't listen to her recordings at Factory School or the University of Pennsylvania online. Conceptualizing how other contemporary writers are beginning to use e-space is also a problem: I tried to explain the rise of the blog as a space for interconnections among writers, but I realized that even the best verbal explanation doesn't fully capture a sense of why and how poets such as Ron Silliman or Gabriel Gudding (in the US) or Heriberto Yépez (in Mexico) might use blog space—for example, by comparing how they use photos and links as well as text, or by seeing how they alter the blogs continuously with new material. Overall, Rodríguez says she's intrigued by the possibilities of using online methods and appreciates having her own publications in e-space. She can mention these publications to friends and readers outside the island without having to find ways to courier print copies of her publications to them, and she has the satisfaction of knowing that she is represented in a growing cultural dialogue and form, with her own writing as well as translations, interviews, and reviews. To date, however, she cannot participate in a fully mutual experience of electronic cultural exchange, use the net to research writers who might be interesting to her, or directly follow Spanish-language conversations happening in magazines such as Francisco Morán's *La habana elegante* (www.lahabanaelegante.com).

For the translator in the US and many other countries, online magazines are a valuable new form of publication, as well as for the distribution of printed magazines and books, although in every country socioeconomic barriers do place limitations on who can access internet publication and how. But for the translator working with Cuban writers, the current asymmetrical access to online publication within Cuba also aggravates a peculiar neocolonial setting that already conditions the circulation of post-Soviet Cuban literature today, as Buckwalter-Arias has described it:

> As long as books by Cuba's best-known contemporary writers off and on the island are easier to acquire for the middle-class Spanish speaker not living on the island or the First World scholar (e.g., through Amazon.com) than for even the best-educated and -paid Cuban, authentic Cuban literary artifacts, it would appear, are primarily for export. Cuban writers off and on the island supply the literary raw material, while the text is elaborated into a commodity abroad, more often than not in the former *metropoli*. The market seems to have picked up in Cuba where the socialist state left off, leaving no opportunity to think about alternative cultural politics, alternative systems of publishing and distribution, about a possible third way. (372)

For this reason it is significant that Rodríguez does continue to try publishing and reading her work in local venues. Meanwhile, she relies on certain sources of energy to spark her ongoing writing, so I will mark them as provisional "third ways" for getting around dilemmas imposed via the embargo and internal policies. Although they are not final solutions to the broad issues Buckwalter-Arias has identified, they are significant to her writing processes and allow her to *resolver*, or make do: her work with *Azoteas* magazine; the writers' workshops at the Casa de Letras; her regular visits to a café near the Capitol for work and discussions (see Photograph 1); her reading, writing, and conversations with visitors at the rooftop (who may bring new readings as well); and the email she can use for followup conversations. She was delighted to be able to travel to Spain for a short reading tour in 2004 (see Photograph 2).

Rodríguez' everyday walks through the city of Havana could also be considered resources. For her 2005 publication in *MiPOesias.com*, she requested that the magazine publish a photograph of her standing in the street with a shopping bag (see Photograph 3). The photograph was taken to accompany poems from *Bosque negro* dealing with hunger, scarcity, and everyday urban life, and it exemplifies her creative use of the electronic journal's space in spite of her lack of full access to it.[11]

Thanks to Jorge Guitart, Roberto Tejada, and Rosa Alcalá for their assistance with this project; to Brian D. Collier for his cover drawing; to Joel Kuszai and Factory School for supporting the republication of this book; and to Reina María Rodríguez for granting me the privilege of working with her writings and hearing her comments.

Notes

[1] Diaz Infante, Duanel. "Isla violeta en entero verde (otra ocasión para leer a Reina María Rodríguez)." *Cubista* (invierno 2004-2005): <http://www.cubistamag.com/stanza.duanel.html>. 7 June 2005.

[2] *Lunar Caustic* was first published in 1963. Citations here are taken from a later edition (London: Jonathan Cape Ltd., 1968).

[3] Email from Reina María Rodríguez to Kristin Dykstra, June 14 2005. My translation.

[4] "La ballena" appeared in the prizewinning collection *Las voces del pantano* (Havana: Ediciones Unión, 2001; Premio David 2000, Cuento). "The Whale," a translation of "La ballena," has been published by *The New Review of Literature* (tr. Henrry Lezama & Kristin Dykstra; 2005).

[5] "Bridge over troubled waters: and view from the bridge four years on" (1996). *The Bodies That Were Not Ours and Other Writings*. NY: Routledge, 2001. 154-162. 159.

[6] Kcho's artwork appears in the national collection at Havana's Museum of Fine Arts, but it is not framed for viewers in the same terms that Fusco uses.

[7] With this commentary I am not suggesting that all of Rodríguez' maritime imagery must be understood in these political terms. For example, boats in her more recent poem "Las sirenas" carry little sociopolitical weight, instead representing anguish. Yet they could have been overtly political: Rodríguez tells me that the sirens mourn the death of Indira Gandhi, but she left out any direct reference to the political leader, naming her only as a woman mantled with birds. "Las sirenas" is from the as yet unpublished

collection *Coger y dejar*. A translation and more extended note on Rodríguez' statements appear in *Fascicle* magazine.

[8] From "Isla violeta en entero verde," my translation. "Luz acuosa" appears in Spanish, with an English translation, in *Violet Island and Other Poems*.

[9] "Reinscribing the Aesthetic: Cuban Narrative and Post-Soviet Cultural Politics," *PMLA* March 2005 (vol. 120, no. 2), 362-374. There were significant earlier confrontations between artists and the state (Arrufat himself was disciplined in the past). However, Buckwalter-Arias notes that state paradigms for culture have been significantly shaken in the past decade, with authors as revered as Nicolás Guillén and Alejo Carpentier diminishing in interest for prominent contemporary writers in part due to exhaustion with the extensive adoption of their work by official institutions (364). Though he recognizes rhetorical attempts to disengage aesthetics from politics as a significant gesture in contemporary Cuba, Buckwalter-Arias himself argues that "the literary imagination and the political imagination are mutually constitutive" and concludes: "It becomes painfully clear in post-Soviet Cuba . . . that neither releasing the literary artifact into the free market nor subordinating it to a univocal and thoroughly institutionalized revolutionary narrative has had the liberating effect these strategies promise" (373).

[10] For specific detail on recent conditions affecting the release and sale of book editions in Cuba, see Buckwalter-Arias.

[11] See especially the poems "Fricandel" ("Fricandeau") and "Comida para gatos o la cantidad hechizada" ("Cat food, or, the great captivating quantity").

Photograph 1. *Rodríguez working at her favorite table in a café near the Capitol area of Havana. It is a short walk from her home.* Photograph: J. Miralles.

Photograph 2. *Reina María Rodríguez in Barcelona, 2004.* Photograph: J. Miralles.

Photograph 3. *A black and white reprint of the photograph that Rodríguez selected for use in the online magazine* MiPOesias *(19:3)*. Photograph: J. Miralles. Havana, April 17 2005.

In Relation:
The Poetics and Politics of Cuba's Generation-80

Roberto Tejada

In Cuba, the first generation of writers, artists and intellectuals, actually born and raised within the social standpoint of the Revolution, came into its own during the decade of the 1980s. Poet and critic Osvaldo Sánchez, in a sidelong reference to Ernesto Ché Guevara and his essay "Socialism and Man in Cuba," addressed the defining conditions this generation would have to defy: "[T]hese 'children of the Utopia' discovered that it wasn't particularly stimulating to be the 'docile wage-workers of official thought.' So it was that in the early 1980s, the State began to feel increasingly threatened by the critical discontent and the political distrust shared by the youngest members of the intelligentsia, whose obsession with turning Cuba's social reality into a truly liberating enterprise was to disclose, eventually, all the moral atrophy and the ideological contradictions of a system based on simulacra, manipulation and inefficiency." In what follows, I recall and rehearse this notion of the simulacrum as employed by Reina María Rodríguez in relation to other Cuban writers of the *Generación de los ochenta*.

Like and unlike the visual culture that was being fashioned at the time by Cuban painters, sculptors, installation-makers and performance artists—a ferociously iconoclastic project aimed at the monolithic officialdom of political and sexual attitudes that were a residue of Cuba's "grey years" (1971-1976)—the poetry of the 1980s participated in the above general revision while faced with its own critiques to wage, specific to written discourse. By the 1980s, the stagnant rhetoric of conversationalism, then the dominant mode of poetic discourse, was seen as a vacant endeavor: one that belabored the indulgent limits of sincerity with its facile depictions of complex moral and social realities.

We can turn to the work of Reina María Rodríguez and some examples by other members of the *Generación de los ochenta* to examine how the poetic address she and her contemporaries forged was capable of countering the spent discourse of a previous generation and its claim to linguistic transparency. By re-reading the work of the *Generación de los cincuenta*—that is, the group of the 1950s loosely associated with the magazine *Orígenes*, especially José Lezama Lima, one of its leading forces—I argue that Rodríguez and others reclaimed a more complex lyric self as a legitimate political construct, insofar as such as aesthetic, social and ethical "location" is argued, be it positively or negatively, at the level of language and its modulations.

Although his reputation in English practically rests on his massive novel *Paradiso*, the full body of work produced by Cuban mid-century modernist José Lezama Lima (1910-1976) is equally vast. The complete works span over five hundred pages of collected poetry and certainly twice as many pages of essays and assorted prose. Written from 1971 to 1976, and posthumously published in 1978, *Fragmentos a su imán* [or, as per my translation, *The Fragments Drawn By Charm*] reveals a series of final inflections in Lezama's lifelong "poetic system." The writing in *Fragmentos* is loaded with images of isolated enclosure and resignation: a veritable "prison baroque." [For all intents and purposes, after 1959, and despite the critical success abroad of *Paradiso*, Lezama's writing remained blatantly unrecognized by an oblivious cultural apparatus, and the writer essentially lived in quasi-confinement during the latter years of his life.] *The Fragments* is often generated by a sense that matter and meaning are incessantly staging apocalyptic rehearsals of "a genesial, copulative relatedness" where "Everything everywhere [is] looming."

Lezama's entire poetic system is structured by means of a wager on the generative yielding power of the image, the severed nature by which language and material reality are cleft as "a continuity that questions /and a rift in response." In his lifelong corpus, but especially in *The Fragments Drawn By Charm*, bodies—often-ambiguously sexed and sexualized as subjects—are rendered meaningful by way of mirror-play; here, the difference between self and other is continually suspended or blurred (the self as same and other), only to be set into distinct motion again, now equipped with the capacity for image-making and representation:

The two bodies
elapse after smashing the intervening
mirror, each body renders
the one it faces, beginning
to perspire like mirrors.
They know there's a moment
when a shadow will pinch them,
something like dew, unstoppable as smoke.
The unknown breath
of otherness, of the sky bending
and blinking, that eggshell
very slowly cracking.

["The Embrace," translated by Roberto Tejada]

The fascinating and complex question regarding Lezama's sexual specificities, both in person and on the page, is the subject of another essay. Suffice it to say that, not unlike the shifting continuum within his work between the high Gongorism of the Spanish golden-age baroque and his own brand of tropical surrealism—where vocabulary, syntax, image and metaphor are rendered both warped and luxuriant in their otherness—so, too, is Lezama in his representation of sexual (and cultural) difference. The literary figure that might best describe his polysexuality of stasis-into-motion and back, or his nothingness-into-becoming is the anacoluthon, that figure by which a poetic statement begins with a series of initial assumptions and concludes with an altogether other set of modified terms. In two of the longer philosophical poems of *The Fragments*, Lezama continually articulates a mobile theory of the image, a constant concern in his work. In "Nacimiento del día" [Birth of Day] he writes: "The body hid inside the house of images / and later it reappeared identical and similar /to a stellar fragment, it returned." It is this bothness of "identical and similar," this simultaneity of likeness and representation, that allows for the third term that powers Lezama's poetic discourse:

The mirror with its silent central
vortex of groped water,
unites images again with their body.
It's the first trembling answer.
Where did the mirror come from,
that aerolite hurled by man?
How did the crystal that breaks into air
without corrupting it, grow dark inside
detaining the image?
There, advancing, nothing is detained
only nothingness fixedly sways.

["The Gods," translated by Roberto Tejada]

An anecdotal aside might serve as a segue into the influence of Lezama on a second generation of post-'59 writers, particularly in terms of strategies employed by a poet like Reina María Rodríguez. The early to mid-1970s saw a renewed but nonetheless ambivalent official interest in Lezama. For Cuba's Generation 80, Lezama wielded a certain mystique due in large part to certain scandalous receptions of his novel *Paradiso*, and to the implications and aftermath of the Padilla Affair[1]. In its wake Lezama was at best ignored or held in check by the cultural apparatus; at worst he was censored and denied visas to travel.

On a certain afternoon of those years, three young aspiring poets—Reina María Rodríguez, Andrés Reynaldo, and Osvaldo Sánchez, to whom the following owes acknowledgment—found themselves adrift in the sweltering streets and passages of old downtown Havana. In an impulse there was suddenly banter about paying an unexpected call to meet the veteran poet, and in the rapid-fire give and take, Rodríguez and Reynaldo impetuously darted up the street to knock at the residence famously situated on Trocadero 162. The two upstarts were met at the door by Lezama himself, who was clearly not expecting any visitors, but perhaps not unaccustomed to this kind of intrusion. The duo unabashedly announced themselves as writers; that they were there to meet the maestro himself. Lezama—tank Tshirt snug around his corpulent body and tucked into his khaki trousers; cigar firmly brandished in hand—asked them if they had read his writings. Insofar as Lezama's work was all but unavailable and scarcely distributed at the time—a veritable out-of-print suppression—no, they replied, they hadn't had the opportunity to read him much. "So if you haven't read me, why have you come? Do you take me for the Capitol Building?" he grumbled, and wasted no time in bidding the minions farewell with a slam of the door as if to punctuate the crusty objection to his negligible status as a national monument.

As I began by stating, the literary climate of the 1970s in Cuba—and for that matter, in many other parts of Latin America—was dominated by the realist mode and expository resolve of what was referred to as conversationalism, with its legitimate aim of establishing a social poetic, if albeit to insufficient effects. Roberto Fernández Retamar and other poets of the largely male *Generación del Caimán Barbudo* (Raúl Rivero, Luis Rogelio Nogueras and Guillermo Rodríguez Rivera, among others) were much less reliant on the image, as they were on the rhetoric of a coherent self and the strategies of the catalogue and pamphlet, teeming with didactic parallelism and tendentious statement; "that avalanche of words," according to Sánchez, "accredited by a militancy of facile prattle, and by an everyday reality reduced to vapid chronicle."[2]

What Sánchez and other poet-critics of his generation have now identified, in point of fact, was Cuba's inevitable paradigm shift, as undergone in various degrees and kind throughout the West and Latin America, from modernism to postmodernism. In the collapse of the master narratives of modernity, dominant systems of value regarding the self, state, social relations and representative modes all underwent a comprehensive reevaluation—or a threefold disavowal of totalization, teleology and utopia, as outlined by countless observers.

This shift can be traced in part to the disillusionment with, and subsequent questioning of, the emancipatory promises made by these *récits*: the dissection and mastery of a purportedly stable self as envisioned by Freud and psychoanalysis; the resolution of class struggle by way of the Marxist-Leninist state; the lack of inclusiveness in both a political and hermeneutic sense, as representation further extended to conflate the symbolic order with the real.

In this, Jean Baudrillard identifies a series of phenomena in keeping with the increase in the technologies of communication, and their relationship with the world of events:

> Simulation is no longer that of a territory, a referential being or a substance. It is the generation of models of a real without origin or reality: a hyperreal. [...] Conversely, simulation starts from the utopia of the principle of equivalence, from the radical negation of the sign as value, from the sign as reversion and death sentence of every reference.

Significantly, Baudrillard makes no claim for the simulacrum as an historically isolated emergence. He situates the tendency as an alternate current with historic antecedents: "Outside of medicine and the army, favored terrains of simulation, the affair goes back to religion and the simulacrum of divinity: 'I forbade any simulacrum in the temples because the divinity that breathes life into nature cannot be represented.'" Despite this historical dynamic, Baudrillard's argument barely escapes the solipsism (or outright nihilism) that allows for no generation of difference, a world where signs of the real are relentlessly substituted for the real itself, where all systems, including the social, are "an uninterrupted circuit without reference or circumference."

But we might make use of the simulacrum in this historical sense, and in spite of Baudrillard himself, to address how some poets from Cuba's Generation-80 successfully deployed the literal and figurative uses of simulacra to make broader statements about the formal "transparency" of conversationalism and the supposed "transparency" of the State. In so doing, we should keep in mind that, despite its insularity and seeming cultural closure, there was a porous feature and a receptivity on the part of Cuban revolutionary culture—this insular peculiarity had been identified and championed earlier by Lezama himself—that allowed the ideas of major postmodern thinkers to reach Cuba, via editions brought back from Europe, translations edited in Mexico and Spain, circulating from hand to hand, or through bohemian verbal exchange or at sites of alternative knowledge like the Azotea hosted by Reina María Rodríguez herself.

In this shift from the modern to the postmodern, of course, subjectivity may be alternately viewed as an effect of language (Barthes), a product of institutions (Foucault) or a result of the unconscious and its endless chain of desire (Freud and Lacan).[3] For Cuba this meant, according to critic Madeline Cámara, that in order to reconstitute any valid sense of subjectivity, artists and intellectuals had "to break down the 'traps of faith' hidden in the books used by the educational system at all levels, including propaganda and everything written in support of official discourse;" the result being "a kind of hermeneutics of suspicion that attempts to delve deeper than the simple chains of cause and effect that dominant ideology imposes on insular teleology."[4]

Let's look closer at how Reina María Rodríguez employs various figures of postmodernity to resonant effect in a poem from her turning point collection *En la arena de Padua* [In the Sands of Padua, Havana: Contemporáneos]. Though not published until 1992, the poems that comprise the series were written from the mid to late 1980s. Her previous three volumes—*La gente de mi barrio* [The People in My Neighborhood, 1976], *Cuando una mujer no duerme* [When a Woman Goes Without Sleep, 1980] and *Para un cordero blanco* [For a White Lamb, 1984]—were still relatively steeped in the elegiac tones of an organized, "recognizable" self as per the conventions of conversationalism. In "The Zone," Rodríguez literally and figuratively inscribes herself in an entirely opposite—perhaps oppositional—locus of poetic praxis. There, she manages at once to suggest an individual and political reality on the verge of outbreak or explosion, by dint of the sham surface of appearances in which a *way out* of indwelling, out of the more diminutive deliverance of the everyday, is rendered, or so it seems, impossible:

The Zone

Tarkovsky

I'm here in the magnetic field
the dense zone where
the grass trembles
bending toward you.
I found my way inside
thanks to the white drawing of the animal
I owned in that other death.
the oracles never come to pass
except in silence
when the magnetic
needle of the aftermath
oscillates beyond us
uncertain   we've walked
under cold rain.
deactivated bombs
in the happiness room
and ephemeral flowers
over fish devoured by fame.
each form has donned its apparel
and now they resemble what they are:
a simulacrum.
but the zone is immanence
and coming back from the place
coming back into focus
the release of each hour

[Translated by Roberto Tejada]

It's in *Padua* that Rodríguez begins testing the limits of how much an image can contain and, by contrast, how much image-making can expose. Elsewhere, in response to both Lezama's gendering of the mirror as reproductive, and as she speeds the otherwise lulling tones of conversationalism to breaking point, Rodríguez sets the delirium of excess into motion in a poem that combines the resolve to assert sexual difference into the realm of the prosaic with a quasi-pastiche nod to the modern Gothic of Roman Polanski's *Rosemary's Baby*. Together, she successfully makes a pointed statement about the female body, and writing itself, as weird zones of indetermination.

> ... I know that everything was very fast and that I was looking inside with a tall, round mirror, which served as a rear-view mirror, and I know I lost myself definitively that time, I was weakening from staying always on the wrong side in the mirror, clinging to my Herman Hesse book by my fingernails. I feel my face falling asleep, it makes me shudder and cramp and I sense that my legs are also cramped, strained, that I have my face and my feet planted in that mirror, and I'm searching . . . where is the devil? and the navel that used to be small, an illusion in the center of my belly, is pushing outward, pulling inward, he's responding to me . . . there he'll be born out of your tenderness and your wickedness, where the devil is always engrossed with the power of the solitude and the births. I cried out, I opened my eyes wide and looked at the clock: it's not the black clock from our ceremony, it will never be the black clock of eternity, but it's not the accidental clock either, the ephemeral one. I've seen myself in the faces of the clock, fuller, more normal, in the time behind the embrace, where everyone is running off to look at the real time, while I'm pushing, struggling, I writhe to find that other time without hour hands . . . just for the insane. but it's not your fault, or theirs, it's the fault of the devil who will also be born from my only navel, from its cavity, from its impatience without a reflection in any unilluminated mirror, in a smashed mirror with burning edges, where I can decapitate myself without desire, or look at myself with a hardened expression, less liquid, less fragile, learning those things about the devil like all of the other women.

[*from* "Mirrors." translated by Kristin A. Dykstra]

Somewhere in between these two limits, Rodríguez points over and over again to a lifelessness, a weariness, a standstill, a lassitude. In torques that explore how subjectivity is rendered operative by language-trace, another poem, "Paradise. Storefront. Monte Street," enunciates—presumably at a drowsy, half-barren *tiendita* or five-and-dime—a ghost economy caught between a kind of stadium triumphalism with the manic droning of the everyday.

> .... nothing specific definable: nothing costly
> the point being not to die not to see
> a boredom that once pertained to light
> stains here and there
> no one knows what of.
> spent   timeworn   nothing costly
> waiting for a buyer to come: useless garment
> my left breast out from under my blouse
> there's a whetstone.
> the rats watch us, distrust us, watch us
> their reddish eyes behind a cardboard box.
> items that meant something once
> simulation. ovation.
> the melody is mediocre   a music blending
>   droning
> to complaints from the fan

[Translated by Roberto Tejada]

This droning brings me full circle to Baudrillard and to the simulacrum, which we might read in relation to Lezama's theory of the image. As I've suggested, in Lezama language and material reality are separated as "a continuity that questions /and a rift in response," as creative oscillations between the "identical and similar," between likeness and representation, where "all things are inclined to a birth, not to repetition." It is by way of this third-term imaging that many of Reina's younger contemporaries were able to posit their dense or encoded critiques as to the "moral atrophy" and the ideological contradictions of contemporary Cuban reality. (Incidentally, we might even consider the material counterpart of this third term in Reina's Azotea, or the alternative space that she continues to run on an intermittent basis from her rooftop apartment in downtown Havana.) Some writers of Cuba's Generation-80 deployed the literal and figurative uses of the simulacrum to make broader statements, as I've already mentioned, about the formal clarity of conversationalism as the supposed window between the social subject the State. Clearly, the most evident figures are those of a failed utopia, regardless of its ideological guise. In "Un hombre sin élite" from his collection *Algo de lo sagrado* (1982-1988), Omar Pérez (1964) investigates how the revolutionary subject (or New Man) had been reduced to an effect of official institutions (or, in his words, "functional seasons") oblivious to the pending storm of social relations, be it in the old despotic bourgeoisie or the new bureaucracy of the totalizing State.

A MAN WITHOUT AN ELITE

A swelling, a subject drunk on functional seasons
a vertigo that trembles the branches of trees,
that's the conclusion of a vagrancy
along the smoldering side of a paradise devoid of intimates
a paradise that offers no other certification
except for a storm of ashes and white hands.
No one knows the exact taste of a face
no one knows and the puffing of cheeks
will spoil any lavish reincarnation,
two faces or a hundred are easy to love
but a single face is unattainable, a fistful of earth.
The blood of those shedding their otter pelts
emphasizes the zealotry of a sun
weakening without the force of its solar spots,
lacking skill, the elites, who corrupt everything,
crack the edge of the stars
on the notch of someone's back, imperfect and unpunished.

[Translated by Roberto Tejada]

If Reina María Rodríguez and others have deployed the motif of detonation, a poet like Marilyn Bobes explores the dilemma of silence by way of censorship and erasure. Neo-baroque in reference and procedure, this poem stems from a project begun in the 1990s in which the sonnet forms of the Spanish Golden-Age poet Francisco de Quevedo are submitted to the surveillance and expurgations of an outside inspector that is the poet herself:

DANGERS OF SPEAKING AND STAYING QUIET. LANGUAGE OF SILENCE
by Marilyn Bobes

Since it is   fierce
if   I say
what excuse
if I stay quiet, who will be able to

But   without speaking to you
        sight   semblance
in the silence
        they say

and whoever makes them happen
and whoever orders silences, understands them

[Translated by Ruth Behar]

As with Lezama, the open, the fluid, the multiple and figurative sense of sexuality and its differences were explored, albeit diffidently, by certain representatives of Cuba's Generation-80. In this context—that is, in a political reality where social surveillance and sexual paranoia have often been interchangeable—Baudrillard's "death sentence of every reference" smacks of the absurd, if not the grotesque. Suggestive of this "unlikely repression" is an untitled poem by Osvaldo Sánchez from his 1982 collection *Matar el último venado* [Slaughter the Last Deer]:

carnation   frost in flames
                                  a wound of boyhood and of memory

let me deliver unsheathed your boreal edge
unabashed of your gunpowder if it detonates and
      I'm injured

carnation   a whicker
                                  a sparrow   poisoned mouth upward
                                  and wet in my hand mouth numb and
                                  bruised in its dream

tiny communist salvation   to tower with
      you
inexorable   lush sword
over our most unlikely repressions

[Translated by Roberto Tejada]

Cuba's Generation-80 had taken a prior call for a social poetics to task and made use of César Vallejo's definition of a poetry that would engage the collective body when he wrote that "the political receptivity of the artist is preferably produced, in its superlative authenticity, by creating concerns and a nebulous politics that are far vaster than any questionnaire listing the affairs or periodic ideals of national or universal policy." If poetry is political when produced in relation to a community whose shared patterns of value and conviction are implicitly affirmed or visibly contradicted—or, better still, when expression discovers those other patterns a society fails to recognize; and if lyric discourse emerges when the predicament of subjectivity itself becomes (part of) the object of inquiry, then the poetics and politics of Reina María Rodríguez and other participants in the *Generación de los ochenta* point out the simulation, instability, and the social structure in gradual halt or on the verge of total meltdown, deploying "the magnetic needle of the aftermath" to show us "the smoldering side of a paradise"—that is, the dissonant exchange-value of the lyric subject in relation to the counterfeit promises of utopia.

Notes

1 "The story, of course, is by now well known. The board of the Unión de Escritores y Artistas Cubanos (UNEAC: Lezama was a member of that board) awarded Padilla's collection of poems, *Fuera del juego* [*Outside the Game*], the Julián del Casal prize for literature. When, however, certain Padilla poems were deemed critical of the Revolution, UNEAC's executive committee found it necessary to pen a letter that condemned Padilla's 'subversive' activity. All of this would eventually lead, directly and indirectly, to the jailing of Padilla, to an international outcry (especially among leftist intellectuals who had placed their faith in the Revolution) and, finally, to Padilla's famous mea culpa: a lengthy confession, delivered by Padilla in front of a meeting of Cuban intellectuals and officials (Lezama was not present), in which Padilla denounced not only his own 'anti-Revolutionary' activities, but also those of many artists." (Brett Levinson, *Secondary Moderns: Mimesis, History, and Revolution in Lezama Lima's "American Expression,"* (Lewisburg, Pennsylvania: Bucknell University Press, 1996), pp 178.

2 Osvaldo Sánchez, "Los hijos de la utopía" *Blancomovil*, No. 49, June/July 1991, p. 4 (translation mine).

3 Ben Heller: "These young poets have embraced the assimilative poetics of Lezama as no other group previously, producing a poetry startling for the density and richness of allusions. Opening up to Lezama was an opening up to world culture, which was a strong statement at a time when official Cuban culture was stagnating, bound to an ideology that was undergoing a spectacular collapse in the international arena. For these young poets, to be cosmopolitan has also meant to read literary theory, the works Foucault, Barthes, Derrida, de Man, Lacan, and Zizek—readings that have contextualized for them the crisis of the unitary subject..."

4 Be that as it may, and despite or perhaps on account of having the proximity of Lezama, Generation 80 poets never fully deployed or

exploited the strategies and effects at the level of language as did an slightly older generation of writers in isolation and scattered throughout Latin America; poets primarily from the Southern Cone and Mexico like those gathered in the 1996 anthology *Medusario*, edited by Roberto Echavarren (Uruguay), José Kozer (Cuba-USA) and Jacobo Sefamí (Mexico) which includes Eduardo Milán (Uruguay-Mexico), Tamara Kamenszain (Argentina-Mexico), Néstor Perlongher (Argentina), Coral Bracho (Mexico) among others.

reena@ceebarte, ceelt, cea

30 cloches